I0224296

The Lord Balfour Hotel

poems by

Suzanne Jones Weisberg

Finishing Line Press
Georgetown, Kentucky

The Lord Balfour Hotel

For Howard

Publisher: Leah Huete de Maines
Editor: Christen Kincaid
Cover Art: Public Domain
Author Photo: Howard Weisberg
Cover Design: Elizabeth Maines McCleavy

Order online: www.finishinglinepress.com
also available on amazon.com

Author inquiries and mail orders:
Finishing Line Press
PO Box 1626
Georgetown, Kentucky 40324
USA

Contents

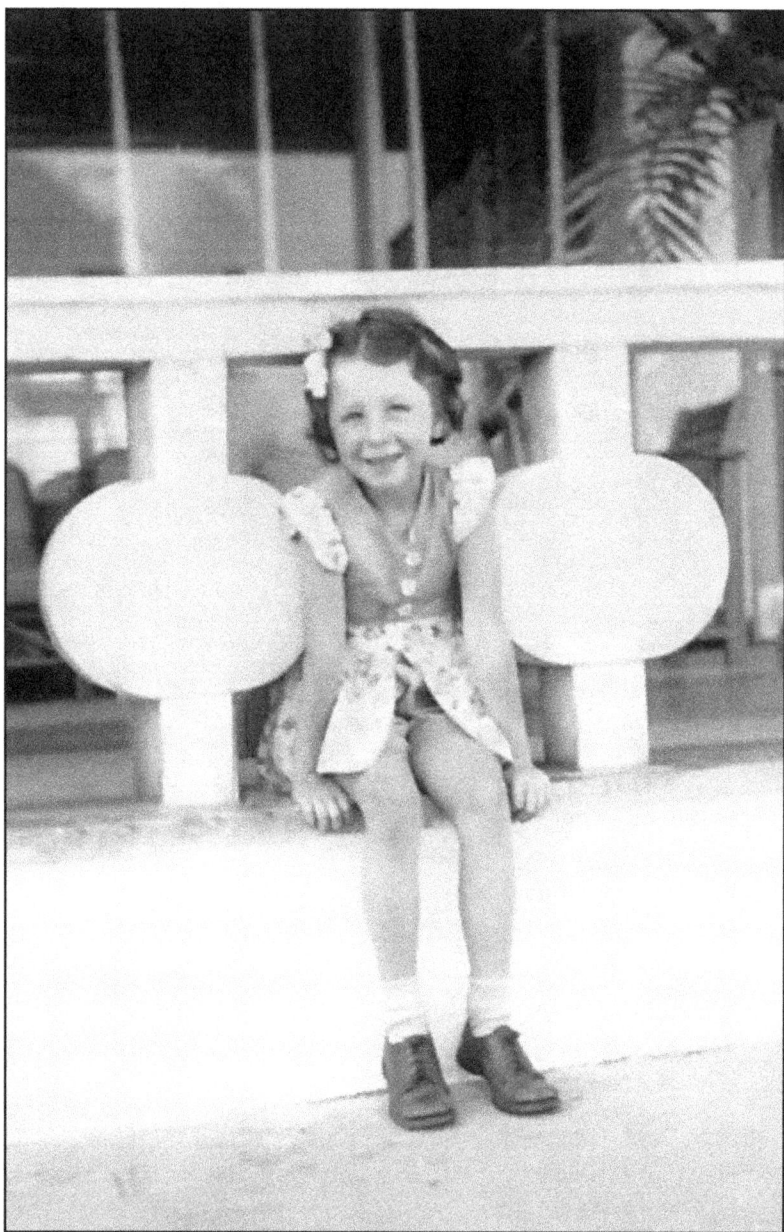

Author photo at age four in front of the Lord Balfour Hotel

Advertisement from La Palabra Hebrea de Cuba, Havana, Cuba, 17 July 1948

THE LORD BALFOUR HOTEL, MIAMI BEACH

Hotel of green nineteen forties
depression glass ashtrays
Art Deco lilies finely etched
on the bright brass doors of the elevator
a mural in the lobby near the front desk
that flaunted pink flamingos
toothy alligators
blue and yellow parrots, royal palms
mauve oleanders.

Haunt of my innocent childhood
my Daddy's big hotel, The Lord Balfour,
he called it "the finest establishment
on all Miami Beach," was situated on the corner
of Fourth Street and Ocean Drive
across from the Atlantic.

Long dark hallways, unending corridors
terrazzo floors in the lobby
and the patio,
an illegal casino downstairs that teemed
with bookies, Cuban beauties, movie stars
Caribbean dictators out on the lam,
looking for their luck in quinellas
taking chances betting
on the numbers and the dogs.

Seventy-six rooms upstairs
came with a fabulous ocean view
where New York mobsters and their boys
flashed long gold chains
on pink sunburnt chests,
then heaved their pale white tucheses
onto a table in the solarium
for a massage.

While some of the elderly guests
the regulars,
liked to chase me
around the banquettes.

When I was five, I wandered off.
I saw a little boy crying
on the beach, unsupervised as I was.
He told me he was only four
and I knew then for sure—
I preferred younger men.

Lacking a concerned mother,
I found safety at the Circus Bar
where Tony the waiter wore lipstick
and dressed up to look like a lady,
and a tall, willowy person
draped over the piano
sang sad songs.
I pondered the meanings.

I remember your hallways, Lord Balfour
long corridors with flowery runners.
Walking on them now, so many years later
I uncover the memories
of an indelicate childhood—
ear infections, a lizard, enemas.
Neon signs that blinked at night
the ocean grey and engorged
seeping into the lobby to scare us
during hurricanes.

My teenaged uncle in Room 207,
just laying around
in his thin white underwear.
From an upstairs room
a gunshot I heard one day
a thud, then a scream.

SOUTH BEACH REVERIE

From my room at the Lord Balfour
with a partial ocean view
I survey the crazy goings-on.
Thinking of my childhood in that place
under the spell of Celia Cruz
Tito Puente, Eliades Ochoa, Fruko y sus Tesoros.

The clanging sounds of son montuno
echoed down its flowered hallways.
Bluefish, pelicans, marlins,
swam the seas nearby.
Coconut palms, hibiscus, anthurium,
bougainvillea, and ficus
grew wild around the patio.

In the downstairs casino, my Daddy
showed off his gun
to impress the Cuban ladies
while he kibitzed with the bookies.
Greyhounds loped around the track,
where pink flamingos postured.
As for the rest of it, never mind.

Its current owners do not know me,
and I suppose it's just as well.
Are they aware that Satchmo
played his cornet in the lounge
in the fifties when "colored" musicians
could not legally stay the night?

The boys who used to wink
and flirt with me on the pier
in Lummis Park,
are dust.
I read their obituaries in the Times.
The mural in the lobby
has been painted over.

THE DRAGON

I

A five-clawed Imperial Dragon
used to visit me in my crib
with flames for breath, and wings.
It didn't scare me like my mother did
but fed me on lily pods, purple plums
red pomegranate seeds.

It protected me from things
that flew and swam and rolled around
moving bats and vampire stings,
bombs and loud machines.
It clawed the vomit from my sheets
when I drank her sour milk,
and cradled my sobbing head in its wings.

But one day it flew away.
Had those scaly arms and dwarfish legs
gone home
to an emperor's palace in China?

The flying beast with fiery breath
that threaded the honeycomb of my heart
and strengthened me
with lychee nuts
and lotus roots, was gone.
I looked at the empty walls,
saw curling wisps of smoke
and wondered if it had ever been
in my little room at all.

II

Corridors in the Lord Balfour hotel
are pinging jazzy sounds tonight
while cunning flamenco dancing dolls
with loosened gowns and lifted veils
twirl on the ceiling of my third-floor room.
I am five, and the hour is late.
The ladies at the bar downstairs
are flirting with the residues.
A transvestite that plays piano in the lounge,
stares at the waiters.
The stuffed marlin pinned above the front desk
smiles at me, as always.

A hurricane is growing,
the windows are drifting out of their holes
ready to fall in shards of glass
onto the street below.
The hotel walls may not hold up.
I hear the ocean howl.

The dragon is back again.
I see its teeth and feel its breath.
It was waiting for me all along in the halls
in the mahjong table's clink and drop.

SOUTH MIAMI BEACH

My Daddy owned a three-story hotel
on a pink and orange island
across from a beach of tinkling seashells
brown pelicans yawning, yapping gulls.
Each particle of sand
a warm holder of stardust.

Flamingoes preened and postured
in the central courtyard
at the Miami Beach Kennel Club nearby
on First Street and Ocean Drive
where graceful dogs loped twice around the track
descendants of the hound, Anubis
lunging for a fake-fur rabbit
shrinking and stretching
their sweating canine bodies
long tails whipping
against the sky.

And the bookies booked quinellas
at the betting office
in the hotel casino
that I was not permitted to enter
although I did so all the time.

My Daddy and my Uncle Sol
held down the front desk in the lobby,
beneath the friendly smile
of a huge stuffed marlin
that Daddy said he caught.

I lived up on the third floor
with my little sister, and our crazy mother
in a corner room overlooking a
colorful neon sign
that spelled out "Lord Balfour"
and flapped with the raging wind
in rainstorms and hurricanes.

General Batista's second favorite mistress,
her name was "Cuka,"
swished and sauntered in the lobby
inspiring jealousy in all the ladies
and curiosity in me
for her graceful bumping hips.
I watched her as she turned and twisted
with the claves, dancing nightly in the lounge
to the rumba, the guaguancó,
while the Generalissimo himself
with a pouty, handsome look I kind of liked
and dark brown eyes
gathered the supplies and armaments
he needed for
his comeback to Havana.

I was a girl, but would I
ever become a woman?
Fear and ambivalence consumed me.
I saw history in the clouds
the future spelled out in script.
I heard the buzz of an airplane.

Sitting on a flowered couch
reading my schoolbooks
in our art deco lobby at the edge of the sun,
I heard the scream of the new moon.
While in China the workers
were dreaming of rice,
on the other side of the world.

MIAMI MIKE

Cool as a Blue Velvet cocktail
on a tropical afternoon,
dusty as the hotel rooms
where you holed up after a heist
under your nom de guerre, "Albert Feldman."
You refused to enroll
at the University of Miami
after high school, as I did.
You said you wanted
to wear a zoot suit instead
and commit crimes.

We never went away together
as you promised, to an island.
But you went there alone
to imbibe the soothing patois of the locals
and avoid the police
after you injured two of their finest in DC
with a gun that was for real.

You'd knocked off a pal
the very day before
who cheated you in a deal.
You soon went to prison for murder
for the rest of your life,
where I heard you studied law books
and argued with judges on fruitless appeals.
Instead, you could have gone
to law school!

Miami Mike, you were the best part
of the island.
As kids we ran along the sand
that bordered our balmy, sunny shtetel
of Miami Beach.

We studied pink seashells
rode the green, moving waves
watched brown feathered pelicans
lift their beaks
to swallow living fish.
We heard the thumping sound
of the ocean, pounding
in every frilly conch shell.
I swore to you that I would never
ever love another boy.

When I first saw you
you were crying,
left out alone on the beach
across from my Daddy's hotel.
You were four years old
and I was barely five.
Your mother was a prostitute,
but mine was just strange.

In junior high when I turned thirteen
and you were still twelve
you politely said I was not the type
of girl you needed
for your current style.

I heard that when they captured you
nodding off, and half passed out,
your feet were moving slowly
in the back of the getaway car.
Your eyes were glazed
and far away.
What were you feeling, Michael
in that lonely dance?
Did you ever want to fold me
into a chilly embrace
and lead an ordinary life?

A SUMMER VALENTINE

How can I describe her?
My mother, also known as Lily
had porcelain skin and staring eyes.
No shrinking violet was she!
I'm planting daylilies lately
in her memory,
or maybe really to forget.

A plant called "Summer Valentine"
appeals to me, with pinkish buds
and an irregular orange splotch.
Depicted in the grower's catalogue,
its blooms are loose and frilly.
I appreciate its softer colors
a potential warmth in mild blue sap.
If these tubers grow out as promised
they'll have the sweetest, strangest flowers.

Then why am I so sad?
I worry that the snarly winds
that swipe across this jagged mountain top
will blow my mother's dust again
into my quiet garden.
And why am I planting daylilies, anyway
on a dry and rocky hillside
here in Pacific Palisades?

In all the shadows
and arcs of my childhood
she sailed like a bat with murderous wings,
darting and howling in the Miami skies.
While I, her terrified daughter
hid away at the public library
seeking the calming sonnets
of Shakespeare, the soothing rhymes
of Tennyson, Rosetti, or Swinburne,
the enchanting wit of Oscar Wilde.

I researched the boxing principles
of Lord Douglas, Bosie's wicked, evil Dad
who prevailed in court
against poor silly old Oscar,
sent him in shame to Reading Gaol.

On those dim pages of yellowing paper
the sharp smack of a pistol cracked.
The Marquis of Queensberry had his rules,
though none were as strict as my mother's.
I dreamed he knocked them out,
all of her teeth.

When she sailed across the horizon
in a purple witch's hat
her sharp, spiked incisors struck
at every waiting throat.
Our childish necks were extended
for those precise little marks.

I ran away from home
when distant shorelines glistened,
and jellyfish and floaters
wound twice around the seaweed.
I stubbed my toes on seashells
jumped over sharp black ocean jetties.
I ran, and ran, and ran.
And now she is gone, I think.

Here on this quiet mountain top
overlooking the unruffled Pacific
will these tubers I'm now planting
bring up life?

THE COLOR OF HYACINTH
for Francis Xavier Jerome Coleman

> *They say that long ago Leda found an egg*
> *coated entirely with the color of hyacinth.*
> —Sappho

Your fragrant blond hair
so carefully combed to be careless
carried the look of a prodigy.
When we were freshmen in college, I thought
you were making a statement
I could not grasp.

I inhaled the coconut scent of your breath
when your hands drifted across the piano
and felt each key you touched was blessed.
But you never stared at my neckline, not once
and sometimes responded angrily
to my thoughts.

I loved poetry, Frank, more than you did.
I worshiped the songs of Sappho,
the lyrical fragments we have left
I was a colorist, a Swinburnian, an artist
not just a giddy devotee of Aubrey Beardsley
despite your habit of putting me down
by calling me "Aubrey," to annoy me.

When you sat at the piano I smiled.
You were a genius, a golden boy
and I a mindless girl, in your opinion.
But I was also your only friend.

My longing to restore the Jerusalem Temple
with harps and flutes,
bring back the animal sacrifices
was not all that would come between us.
I pined for the song of the Levites,
the clanging of cymbals and banging of drums.

While your tireless search
for the perfect human form
did not intersect with any of my desires.
Still, we both agreed
that you were the heir in our times
to Leonardo da Vinci's proportional, perfect man.

So, hail and farewell
Francis Xavier Jerome Coleman
child prodigy at Miami High School
fellow freshman with me at the U. of M.

You hated your name
and our alma mater
and often signed yourself in with an X.
When you became a young college professor
you quickly published three textbooks
analyzing the aesthetics of meaning.
The essays you wrote for the Partisan Review
glittered, along with Susan Sontag's
and the rest of that crowd
who lived long enough to become famous,
while you did not.

I was so proud of you, Frank Coleman,
endearing, but way too clever by far.
Then after all those amazing
early academic achievements, you grew thin.
Your handsome, lissome body
turned into stone in the hospital,
and then returned to dust.

I guess you dove once too often
into the Aeolian shallows
where a sea worm must have gotten you.
You were buried in Boston in winter snow
with an epitaph in the Globe, but very few mourners.
I was in California, far away.

You spoke of the end of times, in the last of your books,
"The Harmony of Reason, A Study in Kant's Aesthetics."
When I told you I planned to become
a progenitor to a multitude of Jews,
you predicted your own muddy grave
where the mourners would never show up
and the markers and spaces
would gradually disappear,
fading away like Sappho's voice
and all that is perfect and rare in this world
would be lost.

A TRANSLATION OF SAPPHO'S FRAGMENT 31

I envy the man who sits near you,
count him a peer of the Gods.
He hears your delicate speech
and melodious laughter
that will no longer stir me
to madness.

Your presence that rouses
the beating blood to my breast
will be his to enjoy or discard
as he wishes.

Struck dumb by
your manners and grace
my voice falters, my tongue ties in knots
a fire runs through my limbs.
My eyes go sightless with enchantment.
I faint at the hint
of your perfume.

But you will sail away soon
with your new husband
to set up a home
on a faraway island.

When you enter a room,
I grow weak
my ears pound melodiously
hearing your laughter.
My breath stops
when you speak.
Will I ever see you again, Anactoria?
And if I do, will you be the same?

Overcome by your charm
a thin perspiration covers my limbs.
I am mute, and when you speak to me
I stammer.

This morning at the gymnasium
I saw you reclining,
you stared at your own image in the pool
my pulse stopped.
I turned paler than dry grass
on the edge of dying.

Your shadow escorts
me at night to sleep.
I hug my pillow of straw
and imagine it is you
Anactoria, so rare and so beautiful
who will be a stranger to me soon.

Thoughts of your departure
the risky journey you must take
tomorrow on the dark sea
bring me to the throbbing edge
of morning.
And when the sun comes up, I weep.
Here on Mytilene
this too must be endured.

ROWENA AND THE MATADOR

The Florida sun hurled rays of brightness
outlining the palm trees in tinsel
when a matador sauntered through
the terminal one day in Coral Gables,
introduced to me as a new connection.
Our chatter slithered and swayed,
a mocha chip ice cream cone
I held on to tightly
fell to the ground and melted.

When evening lanterns began to glisten
he said he was going back to Mexico
to fight El Toro in the bullring
as was fated.
When he spoke of it a second time
and then, a third
I thought I'd do better to forget him.

I was absent from that corrida.
I never went out to see him fight the bulls
in the Plaza de Toros in Mexico City,
or saw the angry creatures pacing
snorting steam in spirals
on that fated afternoon in the Distrito Federal
when the Mesoamerican sun
tipped its rays for him once more
over the bullring.

I didn't hear the cornets blare
in brassy Arabian tones,
or forfeit the cheaper tickets
I'd purchased in Sol
for expensive ones in Sombra,
or imagine I needed to negotiate the options
spirit versus beast, Converso or Jew
or broker trade-offs
weigh my choices, toss the chances,
choose between life and death.

The impact of my absence
was lessened, however
when I asked my friend Rowena
to go out there for me instead.
Rowena, my doppelganger,
my shadow, my loyal alter-ego
who always took up the slack.
What was she trying to prove?
I had no idea.

You must tell me about it, Rowena,
I pleaded with her afterward,
describe what happened—
please say what you remember. I want to
know about the bullfight.
I asked her, did you appreciate
the colors, the capes, the pageantry?
Were you frightened? Did you scream?

Steady in her manner, resonant in tone
Rowena, whose phrases lingered
in syllables fully aligned
with the metronomic clicking of a tambourine
and the rapid beating of my heart,
told me she almost fainted
when the animal entered the ring.

Flipping her Spanish lace fan
she said she nearly blacked out again
when the matador appeared.
Brave, graceful, and relaxed
in the face of his mortal challenge
quintessentially Iberian
a bun clasped snappily at his nape,
a dazzling traje de luz.

Rowena who'd painted my eyelids
in a shadow of silver sparkles
backstage at the Ring Theater
after the last performance
barely a week before, then nearly drowned
in an after-party bubble bath
with my new Mexican connection
gulping soapy waters as they gasped,
continued talking.

Please tell me, Rowena, I begged her
was the matador what they say he is,
half human and half beast?
Did he toss you the bloody oreja?
Did he honor you above all other women
shouting Ole! to him in the stadium that day
with a trophy presentation
of the brave creature's tail?

I know you are beautiful, Rowena,
did he take you out to celebrate
in a little restaurant
on the Plaza Popocatepetl
where they serve a psychedelic
chocolate drink they call atole?
Did he order the Pato con Almendros
with tortillas blancas on the side?

Later we found her asleep in the palace,
dreaming of Picasso, and bullfights.

LIFTED FROM THE SEA

Just one of those barnacled boys,
Roman copies of Greek bronzes
plucked from deep Aegean waters
then installed as a prize
in the Archeological Museum in Naples,
or was it a genuine kouros
accidentally preserved intact,
after a long-ago sea wreck?

Why did he come into our world at all
with a dazed look and seashell eyes?
Did he shake off his blanket of weeds
and cry foul,
when pulled abruptly from the depths?

The statue seemed incapable of speech
its manner was innocent
Childlike, with staring eyes
it only looked outward.

I had just arrived in Italy,
a tourist hitting the galleries.
Seeing him naked in the museum
I was overwhelmed by emotion.
I felt that I encroached
ancient boundaries.

Did this creature of the waters
enter our modern sphere
just to please us
with his graceful Grecian ways?
His face was darkly beautiful,
melodic with silent songs
and a pasted Archaic smile.

Could this be Orpheus,
returning in season

from a yearly visit to the Underworld
strumming strange Aeolian melodies
on a lyre made of goat gut
and a green sea-tortoise shell?

What does this creature ask
from our unsettling modern world?
Will he restore the sounds of poets
lost in Alexandria, or before?
Will he play his sorrowful music
to ease our journey
to the river Styx?

LE BANANE NOIR
for Walter Hill

Two mixed up kids from the South
trying to define ourselves,
in the seventies we ended up
in the City of Brotherly Love.
You said you wanted to be
an artist like I was,
but I didn't know what I was.

Le Banane Noir was our hangout,
that glorious nightspot, so trendy and slummy
with low lit candles, secluded nooks
things going on in the side rooms
that could only be guessed at—
Le Banane Noir was the place
to be seen in Philly in those days,
or maybe not.

I married a cute professor from Penn
although you said you didn't like him.
And Le Banane Noir, late at night
burned down to the ground,
just embers by morning.
For consolation, I gave you
Roy Campbell's translation
of The Poems of St. John of the Cross.

The Club Mauna Loa in Mexico City
with a somewhat more reputable clientele
burned down as well
just after we went there, that time
you flew out to see me on tickets you got
from Braniff International Airways
where you worked on the night desk
in reservations.

Mexico City! It was my place and my time,
but it never was yours.
You said you didn't love me in that way
but I wondered if maybe somehow you did.
And you never understood
the complexity of how I felt about you
when I finally grasped
that wherever you went
something always burned down.
We were each seeking our own
kind of paradise
and Le Banane Noir, in Philadelphia
while it lasted, was the ticket for you.

No one in academic or nursery school circles
saw a play on words in their name,
and I did not enlighten them.
But I was aghast and appalled
that their signature dessert
was just an ordinary banana split
with Hershey's syrup dripped and scrawled
and cream that was extruded, not whipped.
No thick and sweet Parisian fudge
unctuously pleased my ultra-refined palate
nor did any exotic Tahitian vanilla bean tease it.
The ice cream was not churned but purchased,
with cherries on top as red as diaper rash
it tasted to me like plastic.

In fact, was there any concoction at all
worth sampling, that bleak winter year
in Philadelphia?
I had better luck opening tin cans for my husband
and the atmosphere in Center City
was foreboding.

I sat still one evening
stunned, unbelieving
on a flowery, upholstered chair
comforted by my good man
and our new baby boy.
You were absent, not there
and would be gone forever.
Not dumped in the ground,
which might have been decent
but scattered in ashes
on the Atlantic's cold waters.

Can I honor you now my old friend
and often muse,
by remembering your favorite stamping ground
the unholy city of Phil-a-DEL-phi-AH
where you staggered on sidewalks
near Rittenhouse Square
picking up strangers in passing cars?

What killed you?
No one imagined it was natural causes
and the autopsy was unclear.
I said prayers for your soul
every day for a year
and I never lifted a paintbrush again.

HANDSOME MEN ARE CAKES

I think of handsome men as cakes.
They exude a faint aroma of lemon.
First the tartness reels you in
and then the sugar hits you.
If a vanilla bean rings a certain note
it completely knocks you out.
The flour and butter will sustain you,
but maybe it's the eggs.

A gorgeous cake I well recall
was a mocha hazelnut meringue
whipped up with frilly, frothy whites
folded into streaky yolks.
The flecks of cocoa dispersed throughout
contrasted darks and lights.

Another one, I must confess
was angel food laced with strychnine.
Topped with silver sprinkles and vanilla chips,
but cold inside as a bombe glacée
I thought it came from heaven.

Once I spied an orange cake
glowing brightly on a silvery platter,
the yellow glaze melting drop by drop
as hot as the Florida sun.
I cried a heap over that one,
and never got a bite.

But I always, always wondered about
the cake at the end of the line,
until one lucky day I tried
a double whipped cream layer delight
with weeping blue sprinkles that looked like stars,
a cake to last me all my life.
With ten rosy strawberries draped on top
I thought it was sublime.

CHOCOLATE TRUFFLES

I've acquired a box of truffles
to adorn my kitchen shelf.
Truffles of rarest flavor
along with a ticket for more
as long as the ticket lasts.

These are not the truffles
you may have thought,
pulled out from the ground
by pig snouts
in the damp, deep forests
of the Périgord.
These are chocolate truffles,
black diamonds
a far more discriminating sort
and the tragic predilection
of my unravelling mind.

Some are laced with Madeira,
others were injected with rum
a tinge of Chartreuse, Pernod or Triple Sec.
But it's the bitter orange essence
of Cointreau I like the best.

I grabbed the first one I saw
and popped it into my mouth
to enlarge a sphere of awareness
that originally came from an earlier batch.
I couldn't believe those candies
were so much the same.

I recently tried a lofty one,
an excellent dark nibble
as strong as volcanic lava
but sweet as orange mousse.

I think it was the finest truffle
anyone has ever sampled
in the whole lengthy history
of hungry humankind.

Here in this unlikely palace,
on our blue green spinning, whirling earth
I am telling you the truth.
Nothing has ever been finer
than that excellent dark bite
if you are, like me, on a journey to the center
of a deeper, brighter awareness.

My mind's on the road to being lost
I wonder if my attention is slipping
The ground tilts with subtlety under my feet
The clouds are rolling around like geese
I want more music
than the melody can provide,
another chocolate truffle, please.

I sing my weird song unexpectedly
in inappropriate places,
my dignity has washed away with the tide.
I can't concentrate on particulars,
the laundry is going undone.

I am drenched all the time
with a longing
that I hope is not a prelude
to my utter demise.
I cannot control my craving
for the deep orangey darkness
of chocolate, chocolate, chocolate!

ROLLING WITH THE NA NACHS

I'm on the way to Uman
to pray at the grave
of Rebbe Nachman of Breslov.
Life is empty, life is nothing
I can't hide from things.

Why do you tempt me
with your skin?
I am running away to Uman,
singing ancient tunes.

The hairs on your belly,
the scent of your armpits
fill me up with misery.
If I can't have you, no one else can,
I am drunk on
your cologne.

Lilies of the valley, blue oxalis
little sleepy daffodils.
My days are consumed by
thoughts of a flower
that I saw once
in your sidelocks.
Na Nach Nachma,
Nachman Me' Uman
How can I exist without
your scent?

When I leave you
I'll be grateful.
I'll go dancing in the street.
How long will it take you
to find someone new?

I'm going to Uman, with the women
to recite ten psalms, the Tikkun Ha Klali,
I'll petition Rebbe Nachman
to pull me out from Purgatory
by my gotchkas,
if he can.

Why do you tempt me
with your skin?
Can't you see I'm going to Uman
to respect our holy martyrs,
to recall their earthly summers.
I'll sing ten psalms for them
on Rosh Hashanah
near their bodies in Ukraine.

SUGAR CANE

Here in the State of Oblivion
also known as California
I am oversubscribed,
unfocused
in a multistory building
overlooking the Pacific
I long for the hot sun and weeping rains
of Matanzas, Cuba.

I settle out my cravings
with the pulsing sounds of Celia Cruz
I can hear Atlantic waves
pinging on the shores
when she shouts, "Azucar!"

I remember the sweetness
of the sugar cane, a particular slice
freshly cut by the machete just for me
in the cane fields near Havana,
a green tiara of water drops and sunlight
it left on my tongue.
The individual interior architecture
in each natural section of stem
spikes and crosshatches
that remained
when all the leaves were peeled away
and only the rising sap was left.

The geometrical complexity
of coconut palms
rings circling their trunks
that doubled and tripled,
patterns of sunlight above
that shaded me from events
that occurred
below their shaggy fringes.

The humidity of the island
near the beaches
soaking into my lungs.

The comforts of coconut water,
fresh batidos we drank on the run
made of milk and fruta bomba
the ficus trees tall and rampant
growing wild around the fincas
near Pinar del Rio.
The music, the cane fields, the tropical sun
are all small blinking green lights today
hidden somewhere in my mind.

Distresses and sorrows,
bothers and regrets
populate our current times.
But Celia the coconut vendor
Celia the singer of tunes—
her music fills me with joy
and happy grief.

A drummer pulsing shadows on the walls,
a bongo tapping out Yoruban mysteries
into the shell of my ear
when Celia opens the door
Havana, Cuba enters again.
I laugh at the familiar sounds
and once more, I am a child.

I hear the piercing scream of a cornet
floating over the streets of the Old City
that night in 1952
its lonely wailing soared above
the haze of noise and lights
drifting upward from the casinos.

Those days when I walked with my parents
on narrow streets in Havana
where the eyes of little girls, the same age as me
peeked out behind sordid window curtains
all just small, faint pictures now
drifting through my thoughts.

PINK AND BLUE MARBLE ICE CREAM

Do I really want to leave this world
and miss the marble ice cream?
The cream cheese layered sushi rolls
we pick up near Sawtelle?
I crave bright orange uni
wrapped carefully in seaweed
those heavenly cucumber fans
so thin and crispy
that run pale green with a purple streak,
the heated wine, in tiny cups
we alternately pour,
then clink.

All things we love
mean nothing to me
without you laughing
at the moon
beside me.

TO A PELICAN ON BISCAYNE BAY

I watched you dive, bring up
and swallow living fish
when my sandals indented
the sand and two small wavery lines
marked the edge
of the bubbly shore.

Lately I heard you were seen
flying again over Miami Beach
flapping magnificent wings
snapping your giant beak
still holding on to
the plaintive Phrygian modes.

And what of your weird
ornithopteric squawking, muted yowls
warbly cawing,
the calls of a sea bird
floating off on a breeze?

My life curled around your music
as a thin blue branch unfolds.
When you flew away
I heard the empty clanging
of the suitcase room
where vipers go to expire.

I searched everywhere for your cries
looking for a saltwater inlet
where tiny seashells make pinging noises
if you step on them.

Now I stroll the old seaboards
looking for blue throated pelicans
that yawn, stretch their wings,
then plummet
to capture the thrashing fish.

www.ingramcontent.com/pod-product-compliance
Lightning Source LLC
Chambersburg PA
CBHW020222090426
42734CB00008B/1174